Rap Your World

RAPPING Rhymes about Animals

Thomas Kingsley Troupe

BLACK
RABBIT
BOOKS

Hi Jinx is published by Black Rabbit Books
P.O. Box 3263, Mankato, Minnesota, 56002.
www.blackrabbitbooks.com
Copyright © 2021 Black Rabbit Books

Jen Besel, editor; Michael Sellner, designer;
Omay Ayres, photo researcher

Library of Congress Cataloging-in-Publication Data
Names: Troupe, Thomas Kingsley, author.
Title: Rapping rhymes about animals /
Thomas Kingsley Troupe.
Description: Mankato, Minnesota : Black Rabbit
Books, [2021] | Series: Hi jinx. Rap your world |
Includes bibliographical references. |
Audience: Ages 8-12. | Audience: Grades 4-6. |
Summary: "Combining musical rhythms and
scientific information, students will explore the
world of animals through poems meant
for rapping"—
Provided by publisher.
Identifiers: LCCN 2019028404 (print) |
LCCN 2019028405 (ebook) |
ISBN 9781623103200 (hardcover) |
ISBN 9781644664162 (paperback) |
ISBN 9781623104146 (adobe pdf)
Subjects: LCSH: Animals—Miscellanea—Juvenile literature. |
Animals—Juvenile poetry. | Rap (Music)—Juvenile literature.
Classification: LCC QL49 .T495 2021 (print) | LCC QL49
(ebook) | DDC 590.2—dc23
LC record available at https://lccn.loc.gov/2019028404
LC ebook record available at https://lccn.loc.gov/2019028405

Printed in the United States. 1/20

Image Credits
Dreamstime: Aed Gafur Galib, 17; Dannyphoto80, 14–15;
Noviantoko Tri Arijanto, 18; iStock: Adelevin, Cover, 4; artisticco,
12–13; Big_Ryan, 2–3; Jobalou, 11; rubynurbaidi, 9, 18;
Shutterstock: ADudkov, 3, 21; Alena Kozlova, 16–17; Aluna1, 18;
Arcady, 1; BlueRingMedia, 15; Christopher Hall, Cover, 3, 4–5, 7,
8, 11, 12, 15, 16, 19, 20; Dreamcreation, 16–17; Karl Rosencrants,
9; KennyK.com, 4–5, 6–7, 13, 16; mejnak, 6–7; Memo Angeles, 6, 7,
8, 9, 11, 12–13, 14, 15, 16, 21, 22, 23; mStudioVector, 8–9, 22–23;
nataka, 19; OK-SANA, 19; opicobello, 11; Pasko Maksim, 7, 23, 24;
pitju, 5, 13, 21; Prossta, 1, 18; r.kathesi, 12–13; Ron Dale, 5, 8, 12, 16,
20; Ron Leishman, 10, 20; Sararoom Design, 13, 21; Sergey Bogdanov,
Cover; Simakova Elena, 6–7; STREET STYLE, Cover, 1, 4; totallypic, 10,
20; Tueris, Cover, 1; vitasunny, 14; your, 10; Every effort has been made
to contact copyright holders for material reproduced in this book. Any
omissions will be rectified in subsequent printings if notice is given to
the publisher.

Contents

Chapter 1
Rap Your World!

Hey, everybody! What's the best way to get hoppin'?

Jump behind a turntable, and get some beats poppin'!

Rapping about animals is easy to do.

Just rhyme your favorite critters—

like a cow that says MOO!

There are creatures all over, out there roaming the planet,

Animals like Steve the bear or a fish named Janet.

Walking on legs or flying with wings,

The animals of the world? Yo, they're amazing things!

We'll rap about the animals that live on a farm,

And the ones in the ocean—there's no need for alarm.

Then we'll soar with the creatures that take to the sky,

There's a whole world of animals to magnify!

Chapter 2
On the Farm

I always keep my rhymes clean, no need to get wordy.

But pigs are the porkers that like to get dirty.

Rooting in mud, with an oink or a squeal,

Mud keeps their bodies cool, so that's the **appeal**.

Cows are known as **bovines**—they moo and they graze,
Eating grass out in pasture, they have stomachs for days.
When they're not giving milk, they're chewing their **cud**,
They chomp on it for hours. How are they eatin' that crud?

Cows have four parts to their stomachs.

You can ride on these creatures; just hop in the saddle,

With their long legs in a gallop, they're faster than **cattle**.

Swishy tails and a neigh, eating apples from your hand,

When it's time for bed, horses sleep where they stand.

Winner

Chickens eat gravel to help **digest** their food.

Chickens are farm birds, and the babies are chicks,

They cluck and eat sand, but they don't do it for kicks.

The hens live in coops, just laying their eggs,

And their feet have four toes at the ends of their legs.

11

Chapter 3

Under the Sea

Better swim back to shore if you see their fins in water,

Sharks have lots of teeth, and they're looking to slaughter.

With their amazing ears, they'll hear a faraway sound,

And every ocean on the planet is where they are found.

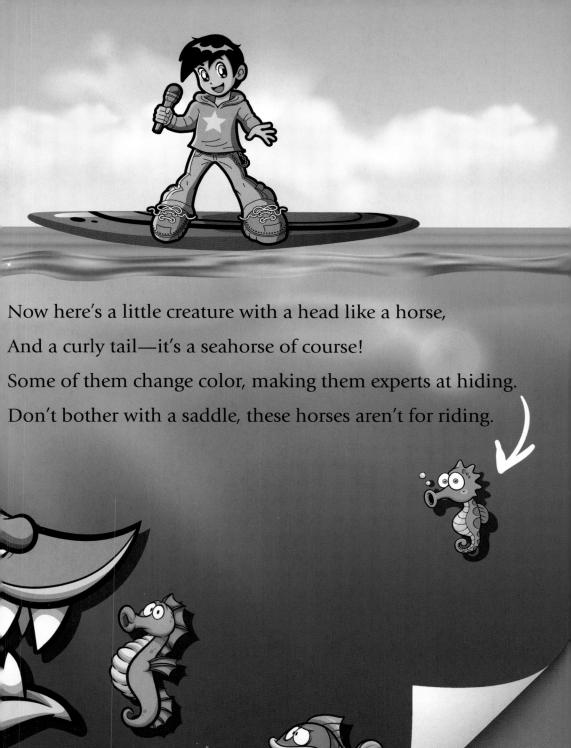

Now here's a little creature with a head like a horse,

And a curly tail—it's a seahorse of course!

Some of them change color, making them experts at hiding.

Don't bother with a saddle, these horses aren't for riding.

An anemone is known as the flower of the sea,
But it looks like an underwater pom-pom to me.
Their colorful tentacles are loaded with **venom**,
To capture their food, yo, that's how they get 'em.

Now let's bring some sea turtles into my rhymes,

These swimmers have been around since the old times.

Females lay their eggs on land every couple of years,

While the males stay in the ocean their entire careers.

Female turtles lay 50 to 200 eggs every two or three years.

Chapter 4
In the Air

Hey, look up there, way up high in the sky,

Watching eagles do their thing makes me wish I could fly!

With super powerful eyes, the birds spot a rabbit,

The sharp **talons** on their feet make sure they can grab it.

Owls are the birds that are said to be wise.

They're silent fliers y'all. Check out the size of their eyes!

Hidden inside all those feathers are some incredible ears,

When they take to the sky, mice are running in fear.

Finches are birds known for their sing-songy whistle.

They like to snack on seeds and plants, especially thistle.

Red, orange, and yellow—they come in all kinds of color,

The males are much brighter, while the females are duller.

Flying squirrels are little critters with the power of flight.

They're nocturnal, which means they're wide awake at night.

Unlike flying birds, these creatures don't have wings.

They have **membranes** on their legs, and they glide on those things.

Chapter 5
Get in on the Hi Jinx

Yo! Think you have what it takes to rap about animals? Start by listing your favorite creatures. Next, dig up some fun facts about them. Try finding words that stand out and are easy to rhyme. Don't be afraid to try and make changes as you go. Before you know it, you'll be rapping your world!

Take It One Step More

1. Did you read the lines to a beat? If you didn't, tap your hand on your leg in a steady rhythm. Try reading the words in time to the beat. How does that change your understanding of the information?

2. Rapping is a form of musical poetry. Is rapping a good way to learn information?

3. Have someone else read the raps out loud. Do they put **accents** in the same places you do?

GLOSSARY

accent (AK-sent)—an emphasis put on part of a word

appeal (UH-peel)—a quality that causes people to like someone or something

bovine (BOW-vihn)—a family of animals that includes cows, oxen, bison, and buffalo

cattle (KAH-tuhl)—cows kept on a farm or ranch

cud (KUD)—food brought up into the mouth to be chewed again

digest (DY-jest)—to change the food eaten into a form that can be used by the body

membrane (MEM-brayn)—a thin, soft, flexible layer especially of animal or plant tissue

species (SPEE-seez)—a class of individuals that have common characteristics and share a common name

talon (TAH-luhn)—one of the sharp claws on the feet of some birds

venom (VEH-num)—a poison made by animals used to kill or injure

BOOKS

Bodden, Valerie. *Finding the Rhyme in a Poem.* Write Me a Poem. Mankato, MN: Creative Education, 2016.

Minden, Cecilia, and Kate Roth. *Writing a Poem.* Write It Right. Ann Arbor, MI: Cherry Lake Publishing, 2019.

Pearson, Yvonne. *12 Great Tips on Writing Poetry.* Great Tips on Writing. Mankato, MN: 12-Story Library, 2017.

WEBSITES

Animal Facts for Kids
natgeokids.com/uk/category/discover/animals/

Animals: Poems for Kids
www.poets.org/poetsorg/text/animals-poems-kids

Writing a Rap – Getting Started
www.youtube.com/watch?v=o6NZoTqWLq4

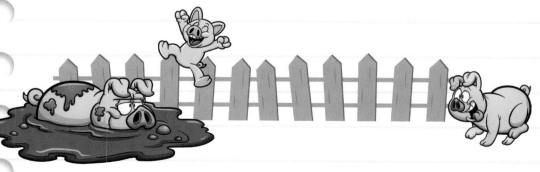

Use a beat to figure out how your rap should flow. It can be as easy as slapping your leg to create a beat. Time your rhymes to the beat, and your flow will appear.

When writing rhymes, try to make each line about the same length. If you say the line and you're tripping on words, it's probably too long.

Editing is a big part of writing rap. You'll make your rap stronger with every change you make.